By Pamela Rushby
Illustrated by Stuart Billington

Contents

Chapter 1

Exciting Ideas!

"OKAY," SAID MR K. "I want lots of ideas. Exciting ideas!" He paused. "Money-making ideas!"

Nobody said anything. All thirteen of us sat and stared at him.

Mr K looked glum. "Somebody must have an idea for the school fete," he said. "After all, the money's going to be used to buy the equipment for your new adventure playground."

"Um, a chocolate wheel?" I suggested.

"Thank you, Liam!" said Mr K. "That's a start!" He wrote "Chocolate wheel" on the whiteboard. "Next?" he said.

No-one spoke.

"We know there's going to be a parachute jump onto the school oval to open the fete," said Mr K. "But we need more ideas!"

Still no-one spoke.

Mr K sighed. "Well, how about you all go home and think about it? I want at least one really good idea from each of you tomorrow. Okay?"

We talked about it on the school bus that afternoon. Our school, Brigalow State School, is very small—thirteen kids, one teacher. The school's on the main road, but there's nothing else around for kilometres. Most of us live on farms, and the bus takes half an hour or more to get to school.

Vicky thought we could have an art display. Aaron thought we could do afternoon teas. Carly thought we could have a horse-jumping competition. They were all okay ideas. But they weren't brilliant or exciting.

Ryan didn't say much. He was looking thoughtful.

At my stop, I got off and waved to the kids. I picked up my bike from behind a clump of grass and rode home. I always had jobs to do in the afternoons. Then I had to milk Daisy. She was the cow that I had raised since she was a calf.

At dinner time, I told Mum and Dad about the fete, and the brilliant idea I had to have by tomorrow.

"I heard about a fete once," said Dad, "where they sold off the school oval in a Splat Raffle."

What's a Splat Raffle?

"**WHAT?" I SAID.** "What's a Splat Raffle?"

"Well," said Dad, "they marked the whole oval up into squares. About one thousand squares. They numbered them. And they sold the squares to people for about five dollars each. There was a prize."

"But how did someone win the prize?" asked Mum.

"They turned a cow loose on the oval," said Dad. "And they waited." Dad paused. He was enjoying our attention.

"Until?" I said.

"Until the cow did—what cows do," said Dad.

"You mean until it—" I said.

"Until it pooed?" asked Annie. She giggled. That was a word she wasn't supposed to use, and she knew it.

Dad gave her a look, but he let her get away with it. "That's right," he said. **"Splat!** The person who'd bought the square the cow splatted on won the prize."

"Wow!" I said. I liked the idea. We could make a heap of money. And we could use my Daisy for the cow!

"Wow!" I said again.

A Tandem Jump

THE NEXT DAY, everyone on the bus liked my idea. Other kids had good ideas, too. Ryan still wasn't telling us his idea.

Mr K wrote our ideas up on the board. The kids liked mine the best.

"We could sell every square for five dollars each," said Carly.

"Wow!" we said. It was enough for heaps of adventure playground equipment.

"But could we ever sell that many squares?" worried Aaron. "Brigalow's not a big place."

"It wouldn't be easy," said Mr K. "Maybe we need a special prize if you sell them all."

"Like an excursion?" suggested Vicky. "Or a party?"

"Yes," said Mr K. "Something like that."

"I've got an idea," said Ryan.

We all looked at him and waited.

"You know the parachute jump that's going to open the fete?" asked Ryan.

"Yes," we said.

"Well," said Ryan. He looked at Mr K. "If we sold every square on the oval, would you think of making it a tandem parachute jump?"

"Sure," said Mr K. "We could do that. Who would be the other jumper?"

Ryan looked Mr K right in the eye.

"Oh," said Mr K. "Oh, I see."

Chapter 4

Ten Squares Left

MR K DIDN'T look rapt with the idea. But the rest of us were!

"Yes, Mr K!" we said. "You can do it!"

Vicky felt sorry for Mr K. He was looking a bit pale. "Anyway, sir," she said kindly, "we probably won't make it. That's an awful lot of squares."

Mr K looked a bit happier.

"But we'll give it our best shot," said Ryan.

And we did.

We spent the next few weeks asking everyone we knew to buy a square in the Splat Raffle. We told them that Mr K was going to do a tandem parachute jump if we sold all the squares. When they heard that, people grinned and said, "In that case, I'll have two."

A couple of days before the fete, we had ten squares left to sell. We'd raised a lot of money, but we hadn't sold all the squares. Mr K was beginning to breathe a bit easier.

That was the day Mr K had to go to a meeting. The local relief teacher, Ms Bertoni, came to look after us.

"How's the big sales campaign going?" she asked us.

"Not too good," we said. "Ten squares left."

"So if someone buys them, Mr K's got to do the jump?" she asked.

"That's right," we said.

Ms Bertoni grinned. "Put me down for ten squares," she said.

Go, Mr K!

WHEN MR K came back that afternoon, we all rushed to tell him about it.

"Thanks a lot, *Grazia*," he said to Ms Bertoni.

"It's a pleasure to help the kids out," she said. "Good to see you're so involved."

"Then you'd better come along to the fete," said Mr K. "And pick up the pieces."

And Ms Bertoni said she wouldn't miss it for the world.

On the morning of the fete, we helped Mr K draw numbered squares on the oval. Then he had to drive to the next town, where the light aircraft for the parachute jump would take off.

"Happy landing, Mr K!" said Ryan.

Mr K didn't find that funny.

A couple of hours later, the fete was in full swing. Dad and I had brought Daisy in the back of the truck and turned her loose on the oval.

Annie and I stayed close to Daisy to make sure she was all right, but she had to pick the square herself. For a while, everyone watched Daisy, but she didn't do what we were waiting for. Soon, people went back to buying cakes, or throwing balls at targets, or eating hamburgers.

Then, we heard a plane. Everyone gazed up into the sky. There it was! The parachute jumper's plane! It came closer and closer. It circled the school. We could see two small figures in white overalls at its open door. "Go, Mr K!" we shouted. We knew he couldn't hear us, but we shouted anyway.

And then—they tumbled out.

The two small white figures fell and fell.

A Wham and a Splat!

EVERYTHING WENT quiet.

Suddenly, I felt worried. Maybe this hadn't been such a good idea. What if something went wrong? What if Mr K got hurt? I saw Ms Bertoni with her hand up to her mouth.

Annie pulled at my arm.

"What?" I said. "What?" I didn't want to look away from the sky.

"Daisy," she said. "Daisy's done it."

I snatched a quick look. Daisy had done it, all right. Very neatly, right in the middle of a square.

I looked back at the sky. The two figures were still falling. And then, suddenly, the parachute opened. Everyone breathed a big sigh of relief. Then they all cheered.

"Go, Mr K!" we shouted.

The two figures came closer and closer. They were right over the oval.

Then, **wham!**

They hit the ground, fell over and rolled. And they rolled right onto the square Daisy had just decorated. **Splat!**

When they got up, their overalls weren't white any more.

All of us kids rushed over. We'd been going to give Mr K a hug. But when we saw the state of him, we changed our minds.

It didn't stop Ms Bertoni, though. She hugged him anyway.

You'd never guess who owned the square Mr K had landed on. Yes, it was Ms Bertoni! She said she was going to share the prize with him.

And they're sharing more than that now. Mr K and Ms Bertoni got engaged. When they get married, all the kids at the school, all thirteen of us, as well as Annie, are going to be bridesmaids and groomsmen.

And Daisy's going to be the guest of honour.